# LES FAUVES

BARBARA CROOKER

**C&R Press**
Conscious & Responsible

Printed in the United States of America

First Edition
1 2 3 4 5 6 7 8 9

Selections of up to two pages may be reproduced without permissions. To reproduce more than two pages of any one portion of this book write to C&R Press publishers John Gosslee and Andrew Sullivan

Cover Art by Eugenia Loli
Interior and cover design by C&R Press with thanks to Victoria Dinning

Library of Congress Cataloging-in-Publication Data

ISBN-13: 978-1-936196-69-2
ISBN-10: 1-936196-69-7
LCCN: 2016950662

C&R Press
Conscious & Responsible
www.crpress.org
Winston-Salem, NC

For special discounted bulk purchases, please contact:
C&R Press sales@crpress.org
Contact lharms@crpress.org to book events, readings and author signings.

# LES FAUVES

BARBARA CROOKER

# TABLE OF CONTENTS

#### four

#### notes/thanks
#### acknowledgements

*one*

## LANDSCAPE AT COLLIOURE, 1905
*~Henri Matisse*

*The last line of the poem is also Matisse's*
*"From the moment I held the box of colors in my hands*
*I knew this was my life. I threw myself into it like*
*a beast that plunges towards the thing it loves."*
    *~Henri Matisse*

This hillside's the shade of grape soda,
lawn an ooze of electric jaundice,
and the sky's a violet slither. The red,
blue, and green trees are dancing, supple
and sinuous, and the leaves are singing, a riot
of light. He squeezed out red-orange like plastic
explosives. *Painting is an act of belief.*

## ODALISQUE AVEC ANÉMONES, 1937
~Henri Matisse

Delacroix said *Banish all earth colors,* and Matisse
took this to heart, not a smear of clay, dirt or sand
anywhere in this painting. Anemones—red, orange, purple—
drape themselves in front of the woman lounging
on the divan, her red-striped yellow wrapper falling open.
The yellow wallpaper, too, is striped, a tiger ready to pounce.
And isn't this the color of happiness? Like the sun
that lacquered the vineyards, filled the grapes, tightened
their skins. That glanced off the sea as we sat in the café,
the one with the surly waiter in the striped jersey
who wouldn't bring us bread, then brought the wrong wine.
But the day was warm, and our lunch, when it came—
grilled sardines drizzled with oil—was just what we wanted,
and we were happy in the sun on the white wicker chairs,
something blooming in my heart, anemones
spilling from their vase.

## LA MER VUE À COLLIOURE, 1906
*~Henri Matisse*

Here is the sea as Henri saw it,
and we have seen it, too, driving
along *les corniches*, the cobalt water
scissored with sailboats, white triangle
cutouts on a *papier couleurs* sea.
Matisse's violent *vertes*, trees and bushes,
fields of *jaune, cerise, violet*;
the houses in town, their wild
paint combinations: vermillion/lime,
gentian/terra cotta, pomegranate/mauve. . . .
If you let your eyes go out of focus,
you could be in front of a *vendeur
de crème glacée: citron vert, abricot,
ananas, menthe. Boule* after creamy *boule.*
The whole world dissolves around the edges,
would melt, if you'd let it.

## AT THE MOULIN PASTELIER

That night in the Lauragais, we sat on the lawn swing
watching the moon's bright sickle slice the deepening
sky, the long spill of landscape flushed with sunset.
From the woods, we heard two *hiboux*: *Qui vous? Qui vous?*
The bands of color faded, smudged into each other like chalk
pastels. This auberge was a *pastelier*, an old mill for turning
woad into blue dye. Here, they dried the plants, ground them
to paste, let it ferment, then molded it into *cocagne*, balls
the size of grapefruit, let them sit for six months. This
was the famed Land of Cockaigne, where all you had to do
was lie on your back and watch your wealth dry in the sun.
How to get rich in the 16th century. And how sweet
this evening has turned, hearing the owls, the only birds
that can see the color blue. Gauguin said *if you see
a tree as blue, make it blue.* Our room here is painted
pale duck egg. *The devil* said Mitch Ryder *has a blue
dress on.* I say the night is equal parts hydrangeas
and sapphires. You say *honey, it's getting cold.*

## LEAVING

That last night, we sat in the village square
at a little café; it was October, not many more
evenings like this.  The magret de canard
was rosy in its sauce of cèpes, breath
of the earth; the local red, rough
in its carafe; the bread in its basket,
where it belonged.  But you're going home,
and I'm staying here, a dry crust left out
after the feast.  Across the street, strands
of jazz spill from the one lit window,
dissolve in the tall cold glass of night.

# AUVILLAR

*Everyone has two countries, his or her own,*
*and France. ~ Thomas Jefferson*

And I say, *vive la France*, especially this village
of honey-soaked stone flanked by the green Garonne,
red-tiled roofs, figs falling fat and sweet
from the trees. Where the local cheese, the *picodon*,
lies down on its bed of baguette. Even though
I mangle the language, fail to curdle the r's in the back
of my throat, can't force the "ehn" in "pain" to go up
my nose, keep forgetting the rules for the *plusqueparfait*,
I still think I'm a *citoyen*, an *enfant de la patria*. . . .
My short legs and flabby thighs have somehow elongated,
and I can stalk gracefully over the cobblestones on shoes
so wicked they might be illegal. Of course I'm wearing black,
sleek as the *nuit*, which is decorated by *les étoiles dorés, juste*
*comme ça*. The scarf that's flung casually around my neck
makes *toute le monde* look shabby *en comparaison*. Isn't this
what heaven will be? Days golden as croissants, God tapping
her elegant fingernails on the *étagère*, welcoming me in,
asking why it's taken so long to arrive?

## PANSIES, 1918-1919
### ~Henri Matisse

Just a jar of pansies on a wooden table, so real
I can smell their powdery scent. Matisse said
*If there's no emotion, you shouldn't paint,*
and I wonder what he was feeling when he drew
this room. The wallpaper, a *Toile de Jouy*, is
that shade of blue that says *France*, all abstract
arabesques and arches. No swains or shepherdesses
frolic here, no picnics by the lake, no delights
of the seasons: spring flowers, summer wheat,
autumn grapes, winter sleighs. The pansies leap
off the table, hit you in the eye. Their sunny
faces nod, deep in thought. My hardened heart
eases, just to look at them. So jump up
and kiss me, O my darling. Paint your sweet
lips over my skin.

## SIXTY-FIVE

*Why would you want to strip off at our age?*
*Mingle all that sagging, crepey skin with another's greying flesh?*
<u>French Leave</u>, *Fidelma Cook*

Well, why would you not? If the lights are dim and the candles are lit, surely this old skin will do, the two of us rubbing along slowly like freight trains chugging up a grade. So your stomach's not a ridge of washboard abs or *tablettes de chocolat* as they say here; mine's a puddle of warm *crème brûlée*. Pears ripen slowly as they concentrate their juice. Brie slumps in the shell of its rind. And both of them, and all of me, are *absolument délicieuse*.

## LES BOULANGERS

Blessed be the breadmakers of la belle France
who rise before dawn to plunge their arms
into great tubs of dough. Blessed be the yeast
and its amazing redoubling. Praise the nimble
tongues of those who gave names to this plenty:
*baguette, boule, brioche, ficelle, pain de campagne.*
Praise the company they keep, their fancier cousins:
*croissant, mille feuille, chausson aux pommes.*
Praise flake after golden flake. Bless their saintly
counterparts: *Jésuit, religieuse, sacristain, pets de nonne.*
Praise be to the grain, and the men who grew it. Bless
the rising up, and the punching down. The great
elasticity. The crust and the crumb. Bless
the butter sighing as it melts in the heat.
The smear of confiture that gilds the plane.
And bless us, too, O my brothers,
for we have sinned, and we are truly hungry.

### FIGURE DECORATIVE SUR FOND ORNEMENTAL, 1925
*~Henri Matisse*
*At the moment I'm completely gripped by fruit. ~Henri Matisse*

You might be looking at her globed breasts
or the round bread basket of her belly. Or the way
her curves repeat themselves in the lobed gold
borders of the wallpaper, the decorative motifs
in the rug on the floor. But my eye is drawn
to the foreground, four ripe lemons resting
in a blue bowl, the same shade of periwinkle
on shutters and doors here in Auvillar,
this village on the chemin de Campostelle.
You might have thought the blue was to honor
the Virgin or to ward off the evil eye, but no,
it's because there was paint leftover
from the woad factories, and its use
could reduce the growth of fungus and mold.
Which doesn't mean it's not the color of heaven.
Or that these oval lemons aren't citron suns.
You can almost smell their oil on your hands,
feel the yellow curdle in your mouth.
The roses on the wallpaper start to sing.

## PILGRIMS

So I'm living here for ten days in one of *les plus beaux*
*villages* of southwest France on the trail to Campostelle,
watching modern pilgrims with their rucksacks, backpacks,
walking sticks, who are following the scallop shell,
St. Jacques' path, the dusty track of the Milky Way,
tourist routes and paved roads. And I think,
aren't we all pilgrims in our own lives, checking in
to the small hotel of the body, paying the tariff,
unpacking our valises? How we forget the body
is a field of stars. The rays of the scallop flare
like the setting sun. Too soon, we'll reach Finisterre.
In the legend, James's body was lost at sea, tossed up
on the shore uncorrupted and covered in scallop shells
arrayed in all the robes of sunset. *Mare tenebrosum.*
Mary, Star of the Sea, Venus, rising. Be our tour guide.
Bring us home.

## ÉGLISE SAINT-PIERRE
*XII-XIV siècle*
*Auvillar, France*

Can God be praised in clay and stone?
Or is this simply man's design, the wish
to grow great wings and soar in arches
reaching up to touch the chiseled sky?

High in the tower, bells ring out, their deep bronze
tones reverberate:  the echoing, the rush of blood,
systole, diastole, heartbeat's rate. Beeswax candles
whicker flames swallowed in the dark above.

We sit or kneel on polished pews, trying
not to feel alone.  I sense the prayers of centuries,
the faith of those who've come before, who told
their beads, who raised their voices up in song.

And though my modern doubts remain, and the sea of faith
seems at ebbtide, these bells still toll: *abide, abide.*

## LE NID DES ANGES
*~ "The Nest of Angels"—sign seen on a shop in France*

But the store is closed, so we don't know what it sells.
And we can't imagine where it is the angels go at night;
do they settle in trees? Or do they really make nests,
and if so, what kind of bedclothes would they use,
gossamer or tulle? Thin wisps, mysteries and sighs?
Or this mist, the *brouillard*, rising from the green
Garonne? Perhaps something tangible and insubstantial
at the same time, like the host that melts
while remaining body and blood, bread and wine.
*Vive les mystères.* Meanwhile, the angels
are amusing themselves with games like Whisper
Down the Alley and Ghost in the Graveyard,
as they sip just the bubbles from their flutes
of champagne, and nibble delicacies,
kisses made of meringue in the faint ethereal
light of the stars.

## IT WAS THE NIGHT OF THE FULL MOON,

and the owls were calling, at least six of them, back and forth:
*hoohoohoohoo. Hoohoohoohoo.* An orchestration of ghosts.
They might have been tawny owls, *les choettes hulottes*:
rising quaver, falling tremolo. Cold. Round sounds
distilled from night. In the courtyard, someone moved
with chalk, tracing shadows on the terrace,
strange lobed ululations. I sat on a stone
talking to you, half the globe away. You
could hear the owls, too. The space between us
filled with spilled milk and moonlight.

# FIGS

*If I should wish a fruit brought to Paradise, it would certainly
be the fig—*
*~ The Prophet Mohammed*

I was staying in a village in southwest France,
trudging up the steep hill to the boulangerie
for my daily baguette. On the way back, I saw

a young woman I'd met the night
before. In her hands, a ripe fig, which
we split. Dark violet chocolate

with a greenish flesh, blood-red pulp,
it opened with a thumbprint's thrust.
The seeds embroidered our teeth.

I barely knew enough words to thank her,
my mumbled tongue, clenched teeth, dumb
as the stones under our feet. I crunched the grit,

my mouth filled with fruit and new syllables.
Even the fog, lifting from the river, that had
no language of its own, began to speak.

*two*

## MY HEART

I want a new heart,
not this bit of chipped
blue ice. Cracked
asphalt parking lot.
Hard green persimmon,
puckering when someone
else wins something.
Someone else is always
winning something.
My forehead
wears an invisible scar
in the shape of an L,
for loser. I need another
heart, one that can help me face
the thin blue light of television,
disasters scrolling across the screen.
Ahead lies the sea of grief,
where sorrows line up like a set
of waves. Their inevitable crash
on the shore. I want more.
I want a new heart, one that's red
and full of flight, like this bird
that's singing outside my window,
the one whose only song
is *thank you, thank you, thank you.*

# SCRIMSHAW

So, I live in Pennsylvania, home of potato filling, cabbage
    slaw,
shoofly pie, apple butter, scrapple, red beet eggs, hog maw,
solid starchy stuff. But when I want to go wild, overdraw
my account, then I fly to Paris, change to a black lace bra,
matching panties. Stop at a bistro, eat oysters in the raw
with brown bread, unsalted butter, wine the color of pale
    straw,
then stroll down a leafy street, wander gardens I could draw
if I had talent. For a country girl, this is shock and awe:
even a folded napkin, a work of art. I'm sure there are flaws,
but I can't see them. I prefer Pépé le Pew to Quick Draw McGraw,
Gérard Départdieu to Brad Pitt, Isabelle Hupert to Kate
    Capshaw,
coq au vin to KFC, Bain de Soleil to Coppertone, scofflaw
that I am. Ray Charles said, *Tell your mama, tell your pa*
*I'm gonna send you back to Arkansas*,
but I don't want to go there, or to Utah or Omaha.
I want to stay in Paris for that *je ne sais quoi*.

## WALKING WITH JESUS

in the Blue Ridge Mountains, eating corn fritters
and okra, passing the black-eyed peas. He loves
redbirds and kudzu, all that green tenaciousness.
He's not so much of a fan of men in white sheets,
gun racks, the Stars and Bars, but he's Jesus, so
he loves them anyway. The gospel of football
eludes him, but he sure likes to tailgate. He tells
me that all the commandments are really
about sitting with your neighbors on a wide
front porch, eating peach pie, watching the sun
go down. *Why are you still going on about sin
and salvation,* he asks me, *when you have all this,
right here, right now?*

## LISTEN
*the first phrase is from Psalm 51*

*Make me hear joy and gladness,* even though I watch
Fox News, see the hysterical headlines repeat themselves
nightly. Sometimes I think the only cure's a hit of Scotch,
amber in a tumbler. There are bruises, cuts, no salve
can remedy. Add to this: reality shows, tabloids, talk radio,
the world's foolishness on display: game show hosts, faux
    celebrities.
Whose woods these are, I think I know, but Placido
    Dominigo
beats me to it, his pure notes soaring above the trees.
Maybe clouds are the only media we should attend to.
They know what's important, that it's all water vapor,
ephemera, subject to the whim of the wind. So much blue
to be written on, or not. Some days, it's just vacant ether.
So flatten my heart, three-personned God, teach me how to
    listen
above the rhetoric, the verbiage, the static on the Internet,
    amen.

## ALPHA/OMEGA: A DOUBLE HELIX

Alter my heart, or should it be altar it? Is this a quiz?
    *Zero at the bone* wrote Miss Emily, as she penned a
bunch of poems, then put them in her trunk. Today
    you can recognize her genius, but they were numb,
couldn't see it for the words. Women, the fairer sex,
    x cetera, were only meant for the domestic
daily grind. Step outside the lines, and pow!
    Won't just everybody shun you? But did
Emily care? It's not like she was yearning to be on TV,
    video, or even the stage. She had time
for dreaming, up in her room, didn't need a guru
    until the world intruded. Enter the pasty-faced minister of
God's holy house, the white church down the street
    that wanted her on the hard pew, what a drag.
How did *love your neighbor* come to this:
    Sunday morning's slow march,
itchy clothing, endless sermons, torpor
    rendering the congregation insensible. I
just don't think it's what God had in mind, the ps and qs
    quietly morphing into zs. Even the Muslim hajj
kicks more butt than this circumstance and pomp
    putting us to sleep. *Seek*
*love where you can find it* should be the motto,
    or else you risk losing your soul.
Maybe Jesus had a better plan.
    No more hate, no more wars, and sure, use a condom.
Never mind the liturgy, the organ's sonorous hum,
    move in your seat if you feel the rhythm low down,
or groove on the trumpet blare, the snare drum roll.
    *Love one another* is the only credo.

Politics, environment, chastity: a mixed up shtick
    keeping you from listening up.
*Quiet, hush*, says the Librarian. *Rock on* goes the DJ,
    *jump, jive and wail.* Your IQ,
running to high numbers, isn't going to save you. I
    italicize every word that's important. Our
souls continue their wayward search.
    Happiness? Riches? Success?
The secret could be as simple as bootleg
    Gucci stonewashed jeans. Or it might not.
Up til now I thought it might be a Hèrmes scarf,
    *foulard*, loosely knotted in a drop-dead manner. You
very well might admit this. Women know we
    exist, if we shop. So cut me up with a shiv.
Wash my feet, pour something sweet on them, like nard.
    Deny you know me, three times. The cock's crow.
Xray my heart, is the blood still pumping, frantic,
    coursing, lub dub, lub dub? Remix
your tapes, turn up the woofers, let it throb,
    blast, make the angels shake their celestial booty.
Zero in on what's important. *Be bop a looma*
    *a love bam boom*, alter or altar, all that jazz.

## THIS AMERICAN LIFE

where Annette, in *Beach Blanket Bingo*,
shook her brunette curls, called
to Frankie, batting her baby browns,
to come over and cover her in Coppertone.
Damn. That girl was hot. Doo-wop
on the portable radio, feet drumming
*Land of 1000 Dances* on the hot sand.
*Fetch me my sunglasses*, she cooed.
*And go get me a coke and a hot dog,
pretty please. How about some Hostess
Ho-Ho's, too?* July, and the sun
beating down upon the roof. Juicy
Fruit, Jujubes at the movies. Keep
the hits coming on KLUV, top forties
radio. *Little Latin Lupe Lu.* Then *Maybelline.*
Your mama said there'd be days like this.
Madras plaid shorts, perky headbands,
ponytails bouncing. Then quiet nights
under the stars, driftwood fires, sparks
rising. S'mores, their sticky sweetness
in the salty air. Throw more branches
on the fire. Very soon, Vietnam
will catch us in its undertow. War
with no exit plan. You're only nineteen.
Your chances of getting out are just
about none. But tonight, algorithms
be damned, the sun's going down
with a sizzle, and look, there's the moon,
bathing us all in its false zirconia,
its dreamy zaftig zero light.

## USAGE

Here, in the vernacular suburbs, lawns verb up
from curb to sidewalk, the active tense of spring.
The adjectival plantings of azaleas, rhododendrons.
The punctuation of small bulbs: pauses of crocuses,
semi-colon hyacinths whose perfume stops you short,
daffodils' asterisky golden heads, the exclamations
of tulips: *red red red.* Though textbooks caution
the road to hell is paved with adverbs, spring
comes at us riotously, vigorously,
with a break-your-heart flourish.
Meanwhile, the house, the one solid noun
in this story, rests on its foundation, happy
to be modified, ready to open its door
to the other noun, the collective one,
that's just now coming up the driveway.

## YOUR

not always going to get what you
bargained for, not in this life, thats
for sure. Take the apostrophe, such a small
stroke, who cares if its missing?
All this fuss and flap over usage,
the headline blaring *Truck Crash on I-78,*
*Driver Found Laying in the Road*; I mean,
we all know he wasnt a giant mutant chicken,
dont we? Their isnt any need to get upset.
Grammars only for the picky, the stickler's,
the cross-you're-tee school teacher's.
At the end of the movie, the hero always
kiss's the girl; they mash they're lips together
in the final seen, as the credits' role,
and the screen go's dark.

## SEVENTEEN PHRASES YOU'RE PROBABLY SAYING WRONG
*title of an internet article posted on Facebook*

Hey, we know it's a doggy-dog world out there;
everyone fighting for a piece of the pie. For all
intensive purposes, I know I'm practically
invisible; no one cares about the fate of poetry
in America. I know I'm suppose to be indifferent
when yet another journal emails me a form rejection
six months after submitting. I literally can't take
much more, although if *APR* gives me a nod, then
it's a mute point. Can we nip this problem
in the butt? Case and point, I have twelve batches
of poems circulating. Heading towards fame?
Not bloody likely. I stumbled on this website
on accident; lucky me. I should of majored
in computer programming, not English Lit/Art
History. Irregardless, I plan to keep on going. So
there's no agent at my beckon call, no editor
begging for my latest. At least I'm not relying
on my income to buy groceries; the hunger pains
would be unbearable. But I tell beginning writers
you have another thing coming if you think
it's going to be smooth sailing once you get
your MFA. The sheer volume of good writers
will wreck havoc on your plans. Don't make
excuses for why your magnum opus isn't snapped
up on the first go-round. Don't look for escape
goats. Suck it up and move on. Because mostly,
the literary world shrugs its beefy shoulders,
says *I could care less.*

# GRAMMAR LESSON

What a heavy load of *should haves*
we shoulder as we trudge though
the thick *woulds*, chewing
our *coulds* like ruminants.
The burden of imperatives.
The chain of commands: *Do this,*
*do that*. The links of *and/or/but/for*:
conjunctivitis. The separation
of commas, semi-colons,
fat from skim. Artillary
from cavalry. Auxillary verbs.
*You could have. You*
*should have. You didn't.*

# DICTIONARY

On this dark afternoon, sky threatening or promising rain,
depending on your perspective, I open the dictionary
to page 748, looking for a word or two to break
my dry spell, get the words flowing again
from their rusty spigot. There is **modernism**,
*a self-conscious break with the past and a search
for new forms of expression*, followed down the page
by **modest**, which the **modernists** don't seem to be,
despite their near proximity. Close by is **modicum**,
*a small portion, a limited quantity*; perhaps a small
dollop of **modesty**, like a dribble of honey,
would sweeten their tea?

Moving on, I find **modification**, a word which arrived,
the parentheses say, in 1603, makes me think of
fortifications, tall palisades of adjectives and adverbs
guarding the post.

Departing via the portcullis on my milk-white steed,
I nod in appreciationto the **modillion**, *an ornamental block,
under the corona of the cornice*. Not **modern**,
but very **à la mode**, at least in the Middle Ages.

But wait, I galloped by **modern pentathlon**, *a composite
contest in which all contestants compete in a 300 meter
free-style swim, a 4000 meter cross country run, a 5000
meter 30 jump equestrian steeplechase, epée fencing,
and target shootingat 25 meters.* It made me exhausted
just to think about it.

Back on my horse, trotting into town, I pass a **modish
modiste**, *maker and seller of fashionable dresses and hats
for women.* Ooh la la.

But there, around the corner, is **Mordred**, *knight*
*of the Round Table, and nephew of King Arthur.*
The afternoon darkens perceptibly, **modulates**
the euphoria trickling from my pen.

Oh, **modular arithmetic**, *where whole numbers*
*are replaced by their remainders after division*
*by a fixed number!* O **modulations**, *tempering,*
*inflecting, changing from one key to another!*

Unlock the tiny cabinets of my heart!  End
this drought,  the dearth, the paucity of words!
Let the rain come down.

## THE BOSSY LETTER R

*phrase from my son, David, who has autism*

The bossy letter R will turn you crooked,
just when you were sure your goose
was merely cooked. Rouse you
from sleep, ramp up the music, rev
the engine. Sentence you
to hard labor.  Dice your zucchini
into ratatouille. Reductive.
Not afraid to be ridiculous.
It can turn picks to pricks, pigs
to prigs, bees to beers. Don't look
for recompense. Recreational
drugs optional. Add rum.
Relax and roll with it. But
beware; on some dark night, it'll
hot wire your cat, tuning its motor,
start it turning: rrrrrrrrrrrr.

# *LIVE* OR *EVIL, RATS* OR *STAR*

What happened when you *renamed meander*?
Did the sauce fail to *thicken* in the *kitchen*?
I thought if I refused to *abridge* my grievance,
the *brigade* would come for me. You may think
there are no *taxes* in *Texas*, but you're wrong.

I'd trade all my *atlases* for one small sack
of *sea salt*. Who *rates* our *tears*?
The more I *grieved*, the more my life *diverged*.
Hush. *Slow owls* are sleeping in trees.
Who doesn't have a *hatred* of *dearth*?

I use a *slate* to write my *tales*, this *prose*,
while *spores* of mildew scatter widely. Do
you *know Rye, New York*? If you juggle
*sacred*, you'll get *scared. Deal*
can *lead* to *lade* or *dale*. Or end up

dead as *lead*. It's all in the toss,
the tumble: *straw* or *warts, pins*
or *snip, peek* or *keep*. The *tide* can turn
to *edit*, in the blink of an eye. Which
will you choose: *heart* or *earth*?

*three*

## LITANY OF THE DESK DRAWER

I believe in the dark desk drawer,
nubs of erasers too worn
to rub anything out, pencils
too short to be sharpened, nibs
of pens, screw-top tips, odes
to penmanship in a time
of keyboards, paper clips
that have lost their u's, slips
of paper with illegible words,
brass fasteners, three hole punchers,
stamps in former denominations,
gummed reinforcers, those little
life preservers, snips of lead, pencil
shavings, staples that have slipped
out of line, mucilage, with its slit
mouth glued shut, all of this, here,
in the tomb of the no-longer-used,
where even the smallest scrap
can somehow be of use.

# DIXON-TICONDEROGA

Sharpen me up like a #2 pencil.
Let the shavings curl on the floor,
let a forest of cedars enter the room.
Make me sturdy as a bright yellow
sapling.  Smudge greasy graphite
between my fingers, smear it into
bitten cuticles.  Scribble,
scribble, smoke on the train tracks.
Bring me straight to the point.

## WORD SEARCH

This day draws the *story* in *desultory*,
the slow plodding narrative of the snow.
It takes apart *collection*, finds the low
haunting notes of a *cello* within.   It sees
that *silent* and *listen* are one and the same,
that within its cage of letters, *hearth* contains
both *heat* and *earth*.   Be alert.   A kind *word*
is hidden in *sword*.   A golfer's *stance*
lies in the *distance*.  *Golf* written backwards
is *flog*.  *Refer* has it both ways, coming
and going.   If you turn *wolf* inside out,
you get *flow*, clear water running down
to the sea, beside which sheep
may safely graze, by the *desultory*
waters, on the *earth*.

# FENESTRATION
*an anagram poem*

Where should we place the windows? I don't know where
to start. All I know is, I need light, like the spike of an avocado
rising from stone. Then there's the space the surgeon creates
in the bony inner ear to restore hearing, let a person hear tones
that've been muffled for years. Or the pore, the tear
in a membrane that lets gases pass, restores
equilibrium. The dark spaces in the soul, lost in the forest
of grief. Even there, light filters through the leaves, faster
than the eye can glimpse. Relentless, it strafes
the shadows, hits the duff. Doesn't leave it up to fate
or luck. Without intent, it shines on every one.

## SINS OF OMISSION

*Field of Screams features four attractions. . . including*
*The Nocturnal Wasteland, a true trail of error.*
*The Allentown Morning Call, October 30, 2014*

It's a true tale of error all right, those things we lack:
apostrophes disappearing in contractions (it's) or
appearing in possessives (its). Or vice versa—
American English, such a tricky bitch.
If it belongs to me, I'll lasso it in with a tiny slash:
Barbara's book. Don't get me started on *your* vs. *you're*.
Or slippery ellipses. Now, watch these letters as they slip away
into the darkness:  Field of Creams. Nightmare on Elm Treat.
The Monster Ash. Highway to Ell. Night of the Living Ed.

# LIFE

This is what life does. It hits you like a stone
through the window in the form of a phone call
from your son-in-law who says your daughter's
water has broken too early, and she's in the hospital
in antenatal care. It flips you back to forty years ago,
when your first child was "born asleep," as it read
on a gravestone in Ireland. But life also gives you a car
and a tank full of gas, so you can drive to the city
to see her again and again for three long weeks.
Your grandson turns this into a quest: Big Green Dinosaur.
Stone Jesus. The Bridge. Gold Dome. Ben Franklin's Kite.
Lincoln on the Wall. White Greek Temple. The Swirl,
aka, the parking garage. And life gives you dollars
for the machine, which you gladly pay, hoping
you don't need to save coins for Charon, not yet, not now.
Your daughter is miserable, and scared. But every day
is money in the bank. The babies in the NICU are so small.
Some of them don't make it. Life shrugs. No skin off his teeth.
It's all a coin toss. Then one night, some switch is flipped,
and whoosh, here comes Caitlin Isabella, out in nine minutes.
It could have been a hundred years ago, when babies this small
didn't survive. But it isn't, it's now, and she's claimed us
with her dark-eyed stare. Sometimes you put your coins
in the slot, and it's cherries! cherries! cherries! Goodness
has nothing to do with it. Look at this little one
with her fleeting smile, the thinnest of commas.
Which could have been an ellipsis, but isn't . . . .

## THE RECENT DEAD

What is this glimmer and flit in the tree tops?
I catch a flash of gold, peaky cap, black mask:
Cedar Waxwings. There must be fifty of them,
little jolts of light, filling the bare limbs
with muted color, then flocking down
to the bittersweet, the crab apples, the hollies—
any berries, no matter how dried-up and frost-
hardened, will do.  Food for the journey.  Little souls,
with your prayer shawls of yellow
fringe, your blood-red blot of sealing wax
on each wing. Are you ferrying across
the newly-departed—Vinnie, handsome
as a movie star at ninety-five; Auntie Kay,
whose booze-soaked fruitcakes were legendary;
Angelo, who landed on a Normandy beach,
marched to Paris with the rest of the Infantry,
and made the best sausages in Boston; and Linnea,
whose burden of a body was as heavy as yours
are light?  Or is this too much to read into the flicker
of wing beats, hollow bones, bright eyes?  The trees
are alive with these stubs of small wax candles,
an altar of votives. While you perch, golden acrobats,
on branches and twigs, hang upside down, dart and teeter,
filling in the empty trees with flutter and light.

## IN KING OF PRUSSIA

Sitting here watching the snow slip from pines, no rush,
just blue jays going back and forth to the feeders, the hush
when the world is muffled up in white. Airbrush
the scruffy lawn—that's what the snow does, whoosh—
erasing bare patches, motley weeds. The opposite of lush,
a season of meager, everything holding its breath, the thrush
yet to return, flute its *ee oh lay* in the woods. Sunrise's flush
seems promising, but spring is reluctant, like cornmeal mush
that won't set up, a bud that won't open, a gush
of water stuck in a frozen tap. Listen, I need some color: blush
of a rose, redbird in the underbrush, face cards in a royal
     flush,
or, if it just comes down to dust, the lurid glow of Orange
     Crush.

## THE BEAUTY TARP
*after a dyslexic reading of "The Beauty Trap," by David Kirby*

The beauty tarp is rolled out by the linesmen at Wimbledon
to protect the grass when rain necessitates a delay. Up in the
stands, women are protected from inclemency
by their broad-brimmed hats of finely-woven straw.
It's not only inclement, but downright infelicitous
for precipitation to pour down, spoiling this late June day.
We should be dipping our strawberries into Devonshire cream.
We should be sipping champagne in tall flutes, wrapped
in damask, carried in a wicker hamper. I've been hampered
all my life by my lack of beauty, or rather, by its loss.
Why can't I have the skin I came in with, peachy, unlined?
What is this jiggly stuff under my arms, the wobble
on my thighs, the blue veins mapping my calves like a fine
Stilton? Why can't I be taller, thinner, richer?
Roll out the beauty tarp, I say! Cover every blot,
each small imperfection. I want the world uncurled,
scrolled back again to Eden: green, green, green.

## AGAINST UNDERSTATEMENT: A GHAZAL

*Too much of a good thing is wonderful*
*~Mae West*

She said, pile it on, like a schmear on a bagel,
sky-high Nova lox, a lite beer on the table.

Forget understatement, nuance, shades of gray.
Be over-the-top, like faux cashmere or sable.

Go strut what you've got, be like Cher, Beyoncé,
though your bony rear isn't perfect as Grable's.

Don't match it, but mix it, then try on moiré;
do denim and hang chandeliers in your stable.

Drip glitz, then add glamour, create a display:
red carpet, tiara, a premiere on cable.

Be hot, well, why not, kind of ultra risqué.
Go on, gild the lily, no Anne of Green Gables.

So fling on the bling, and then flaunt diamanté.
Here's more, pour it on, use a Staffordshire ladle.

Mae West crooks her finger, wears silk décolleté.
Croons, *Flattery will get you in everywhere, Mable.*

## COMPARE & CONTRAST

When I was an undergraduate, I thought it
would be brilliant to write my compare &

contrast paper on the Maidenform three-way stretch
girdle and the three branches of US government:

executive, legislative, judicial.
I somehow worked in power panels

and breathable mesh, control
and flexibility, checks and balances.

And this makes me think about two women
from church, raised on hot bacon dressing,

potato filling, donuts fried in lard, talking
about how they got stuck in their Spanx

in a dressing room at Macy's— But back
to the paper, written in the sixties,

on a manual typewriter (an object
preceding the word processor that went

ding when you reached the end of a line.
You had to do the hard return yourself,

with a silver lever) before any shots
were fired over the prow in the sexual

revolution. Then we got liberated,
went braless, girdleless, shoeless. . . .

But where are we now, in a world that
sneers if our waists pop out in muffin tops?

Has the world spun out of control, or is it spun
out of Lycra? We've raised our consciousness

and hemlines, but now the elastic waistband's come
full circle, and we're stuffed into our shapewear

like my Uncle Angelo making *da sausiche*, grinding
plump rumps, adding spices, stuffing the mixture

into casings. Some with fennel, some with cheese. How
do we feel, encased in Power Panels? Empowered

or corseted? Should we go Slim Cognito? Pray
to a Super Higher Power? Start speaking in tongues,

waving our arms above our heads (no slippage here),
shouting Bra-lelluhjah, amen, amen?

# WOMEN

It's tough being a woman, feeling you're an object to be
    bought,
an elusive quarry, something to be chased and caught,
when you know you're more than that. So pull me a draught,
Charlie, give me something dark and frothy. Wars have been
    fought
for less— I came in wondering what a girl's got
to do to get herself noticed? I mean, I'm so hot,
I could melt neon. You want my number? Well, jot
it down, big boy. I won't call you. I have a karaoke slot
at nine pm; I'm thinking a Madonna medley will do. Lots
of water under *this* dam. I want to be a player, not a mascot.
I want something bathed in dark chocolate, with a nougat
center. I want a lobster in my steaming pot,
champagne on ice, and two chairs by a wrought
iron table on a terrace in France. Whoever sought
the fountain of youth can forget it. The lies the movies
    taught?
They're a crock, a foolish dream, a vicious plot.
Life isn't fair, you've got to play your cards, no matter what.
I could have been Dean of Women, a cover girl. An exot-
ic dancer at a go-go bar. Or married to a guy with a yacht.
But I'm not. So pour me another shot of Jack, O Great Zot.

## SO, THIS GUY I KNOW CHALLENGES ME TO WRITE A POEM

on engineering, which is crazy, because I had to drop
physics in high school, got a D in Calc in college.
His requirements: use a solar panel, a conduit,
and a piston. Sounds like a joke looking for a punch line:

a piston and a conduit walk into a bar. . . .
But hey, it's an assignment, so I Google pistons,
find that they're: *an operating part of the disc brake*
*system, necessary to the four-stroke combustion engine,*

*also used in brass instruments: trumpet, tuba, cornet . . . .*
And then there's sex, where something expands,
gets hot, finds its way back home. . . .
Our home is topped by solar panels: photo

voltaic cells that change sunlight into electricity,
a form of renewable energy. Like good sex,
the more you do it, the more you want to do it
again. Praise the rays! Let the sun shine in.

Now for a conduit: *a pipe for conveying fluids,*
*a tube for enclosing electrical wires, a means*
*by which something is transmitted, a fountain.*
This is too darned obvious. So let's just go back

to bed, O my darling. Maybe I'll get your motor
running, the pistons firing in all four gears. Maybe
you can conduct some current, get a charge out of me.
Maybe, together, we can make the sun come up.

## WHY I LOVE BEING MARRIED TO A CHEMIST

Because he can still cause a reaction in me
when he talks about SN2 displacements,
amines and esters looking for receptor sites
at the base of their ketones.  Because he lugs
home serious tomes like *The Journal of the American
Chemical Society* or *The Proceedings of the Society
of the Plastics Industry*, the opposite of the slim volumes
of poetry with colorful covers that fill my bookshelves.
Because once, years ago, on a Saturday before our
raucous son rang in the dawn, he was just
standing there in the bathroom, out of the shower.
I said *Honey, what's wrong?* and he said *Oh,
I was just thinking about a molecule.*

Because he taught me about sublimation, how
a solid, like ice, can change straight to a gas
without becoming liquid first.  Because even
after all this time together, he can still
make me melt.

## WEATHER SYSTEMS

Sugar maples, little fires in the trees, every blazing gradation
of orange to red, and this makes me think of you, the way
you press the long length of your body against me, the heat
seeping through flannel, my own private furnace.
If my hands and feet had a color, it would be blue.
From November until May, I cannot get warm.
Even my bones have cores of ice. But you
are a house on fire, an internal combustion system,
Sriracha sauce/jalapeño poppers/Thai curry. I stay up
late, read until you're asleep, so I can slip my icy feet,
frozen toes, under the smoldering log of your torso.
Even in the dark, you radiate. I am a cold front, a polar low
coming down from the arctic. And you, why you,
you're the sun.

*four*

## THE TURNING ROAD, L'ESTAQUE, 1906
### ~André Derain

Here, the banana peel road slips down
to the sea, and crazy trees undulate,
wave their red and blue branches.
Shadows pool, electric eel blue.
Look, a parrot has molted its feathers,
dropped them all over the ground.
So let's boogaloo down this road
paved in sunlight. Let's dance
the tango, and turn up the voltage.
Let's commit an act of spontaneous
combustion. Let's all go down
in flames.

## OLEANDERS, 1888
~Vincent Van Gogh

He thought oleanders were life-affirming,
didn't know they were poisonous, like
that mean girl in high school with the caustic
tongue, her ability to slip a knife to the ribs
when you'd least expect it. I've met her again
in other guises in this writing life. For Vincent,
the color yellow meant sun, health, happiness,
and look, in the left hand corner, there's a copy
of Zola's *Le Joie de Vivre* with its glowing
yellow cover. Zola, Cézanne's childhood friend,
who's waiting just outside the frame, preparing
to stab him in the back with a venomous review.
Behind the creamy pink and white flowers,
the paint on the wall spreads its acid, grins.

### EARS OF WHEAT, 1890
*~Vincent Van Gogh*
*I tried to paint the sound of the wind in the ears of wheat.*
*~letter to Paul Gauguin*

There is nothing here but wheat, no blade
too slight for his attention:  long swaying
brush strokes, pale greens, slithery yellows,
the hopefulness of early spring. *All grass*
*is flesh*, says the prophet.  Here, there are no
gorgeous azures stamped with almond blossoms,
no screaming sky clawed with crows, no sunflowers
roiling gold and orange, impasto thick as Midi sunlight.
His brush herringboned up each stalk, the elemental
concerns of sun, rain, dirt, while his scrim of pain receded
into the underpainting.  He let the wind play
through the stems like a violin, turning the surface
liquid, a sea of green, shifting eddies and currents.
No sky, no horizon; the world as wheat.

## *FIELD WITH WHEAT STACKS*
*~ Vincent Van Gogh*

He fell in love with a simple field
of wheat, and I've felt this way, too;
melted, like a pool of mint chip
ice cream, foolishly in love,
even though we know
how it turns out in the end:
snicked by the scythe, burnt
in the furnace of the August
sun, threshed, separated, kernel
from chaff.  But right now,
it's spring, and the wheat aligns
in orderly rows:  Yellow green.
Snap pea.  Sage.  Celadon.
His brush strokes pile on,
wave after wave, as the haystacks
liquefy, slide off the canvas,
roll on down to the sea.

**INK**

*The last line is a quote of Van Gogh's.*
*~ Vincent Van Gogh: The Drawings,*
*Metropolitan Museum of Art, 2005*

He cross-hatched the patchwork fields
of Arles, the farmhouses and gardens
of Auvers, trees in winter, the scratchy
awns of wheat fields.  These were the bones
of the paintings, the things that came before.
Paper and ink, cheaper than canvas and paint.
He sketched the subject, then he painted it,
then drew it all over again from the painting
so he could send it to his brother in a letter.
Repetition and refrain.  Slant parallel lines,
to catch the rain.  Thatched cottages, tangled vines.
Sometimes, he traced his own drawing onto the canvas,
keeping the structure. Sometimes, he added more sky.
They were never quite the same.  Fence, haystack,
reed, and rush. *Drawing is the root of everything*

## DREAMING ON PAPER
*~ Vincent Van Gogh: The Drawings*
*Metropolitan Museum of Art, 2005*

Using a reed pen on large sheets of paper,
he translated sky, rocks, fields into dots,
jabs, scratches.  They try to catch the wind
in olive branches, the gnarled trunks, the way
the light lay down.  You can sense color,
though it isn't there:  brown earth, yellow grain,
blue sky.  In thousands of letters, drawings, diaries,
Van Gogh labored with paper and ink.
He made peace with his own awkwardness, using
reeds from the Midi fields sharpened into pens.
Each could only hold a little bit of ink at a time,
so he devised his own notation, a kind of Morse code,
which he varied again and again. As he reinvented
drawing, he found himself.  By the time
he was in the asylum at St. Rémy, he was drawing
everything: nesting curls for the flickering flames
of the cypresses, *a splash of black in a sunny landscape*;
the farmyards of Auvers; clouds that billowed
in staccato lines. Right before he shot himself, he told
Theo, *I still love art and life very much*.  Finally,
he'd found how to make the hardest thing
he had ever tried look easy.  And then,
the wheat field, with crows.

## THE FLOWERING ORCHARD, 1888

*- Vincent Van Gogh*

*Nature here is extraordinarily beautiful. Everywhere and over all the vault of the sky is a marvelous blue, and the sun sheds a radiance of pale sulfur that is soft and lovely. What a country!*
*- letter to Theo*

There's a rake resting against a tree,
and it looks like its teeth have combed
the landscape, straightened out the unruly
grass, the wildflowers, the trees in the distance,
making orderly parallel lines. But the orchard
itself is in the middle ground: wild diagonals,
flailing limbs, branches this way and that. A metaphor,
perhaps, for how nature resists pruning, trimming,
reverts to the old ways. In the canopy, the foliage,
tender shades of early spring, refuses to be delineated,
goes for the blur. A scythe is wedged in the crotch
of the largest tree, pointing toward earth. The sky's
pale luminescence, like butter, spreads over everything,
the eternal sunshine of an April day. What a country
indeed. I want to be bathed in this radiance,
live here in a corner of the picture, raise
my face to the glow like the overhead light
in my mother's kitchen, and never grow old.

## L'ATELIER ROSE, 1911
*~Henri Matisse*
*I came back to Paris free of the Louvre's influence*
*and heading for color.*
*~Henri Matisse*

It's like being back in the womb, isn't it, these walls of pink,
this floor one rose shade deeper? I think about my middle
daughter, five months pregnant. Her baby's grown
from an orange seed to a green olive to a plum. Now
it's the size of a boneless chicken breast. What is it
about babies that makes us think of food? And what
is it about this color that makes us think of health?
Because we say *in the pink* when we're feeling fine?
Because roses blush in different shades? Because some
kir drizzled in Champagne makes it *royale*? But

if you get a pink slip, you've been canned, and watch
out for those elephants on parade. No one aspires
to a pink collar job. And no girl wants a bunch
of carnations, smelling of cloves and maiden aunts.
The sunset pinkens the sky in the west, and I'm
tickled pink, thinking of you. Matisse's studio glows,
suffused in light, the inside of a satin slipper. Pink
the edges of my heart, cut them into scallops, make
them whirly. Imagine strawberry ice cream, rhubarb
compote, candy hearts. This sweet, sweet world.

## SKETCH FOR 'LE BONHEUR DE VIVRE,' 1905
### (The Happiness of Life)
#### ~Henri Matisse

So, this is a schematic, a long smear of teal on the left,
soft greens, synthetic blues, glowing golds mixed with
hard mineral pinks filling out the rest of the frame. Later,
this sketch will realize itself into a scene of bathers, serpentine
art nouveau curves lounging on the yellow lawn, the tropical
jungle foliage exploding behind them. But who can describe
the color of happiness? Could it be days like this, clear,
mellow, no fogs of loss creeping in? Days when not much
happens, the October sun coaxing gold from the leaves,
the earth turning one more notch? Let the busy world spin.
Let me sit here as the afternoon ripens. If happiness is a color,
let it be tactile, tangible, something I can eat with a spoon.
Because all too soon, there will be Death, sitting
in the corner, nursing his cognac. Let me lick up
all the sweetness while I can.

## THE GREEN BLOUSE, 1919
*~Pierre Bonnard*

In this interior, a girl with a blouse the color of summer
sits in front of a window. Behind her, a curtain
falls, a shower of light, and behind that, the tropical
foliage of Le Cannet. Outside my window in Virginia,
it's a day still trying to make up its mind—dregs of snow
in the corners, daffodils ringing bravely in the cold wind.
Spring is late this year, the grass undecided if it should
take a pass, stay sleeping, rolled up in its patchy old coat.
But there are two blue jays at the feeding table, and they
aren't fooled by the bare trees, the blossoms reluctant
to unfold. They know the sun by its angle, see that the stars
have gathered in their spring flocks. They are bluer
than the sky, and they know it. Every day,
there's another cup of sunlight. They tilt
back their heads, and they drink it all in.

## LANDSCAPE WITH STARS, 1905-08
### ~Henri-Edmond Cross

Short broken brush strokes,
cobalt / egg yolk / thinned-out
black, the starry night sky
in the south of France.
Here, in Virginia, far above
my head, little bits of butter
sizzle in night's cold cast iron
skillet. The Milky Way's
almost so close you could
walk on it, follow the stepping
stones, where everyone
you've ever loved is waiting.
But gravity has pinned you
to the dew-soaked grass. Up
above, the stars continue
to pulse, to dance. And look,
here are our old friends, Orion
and Cassiopeia. . . .

## THE JETTY AT CASSIS, OPUS 198, 1889
*~Paul Signac*

Signac and Seurat made up Divisionism:
not mixing paints on a palette, but dotting
pure pigments in a flurry of tiny specks,
letting the colors blend in the eye.
So here is the port of Cassis, where
we hiked the Calenques and had dinner
one night, even though our luggage
took a different trip. *Ça n'importe pas.*
But in this Cassis on the canvas, a blizzard
of color has fallen in the night, dense
flakes of orange, blue, and white
accumulating on the shore, a squall
of ultramarine, jade, and emerald
flecking the sea. Everywhere,
hundreds of little brush strokes,
birdseed thrown at the sky.
And you and I, in that small hotel,
no pajamas, toothbrushes, change
of clothes. Nothing to wear
to bed that night but ourselves.
And so you painted kisses
all over my breasts, while
I blended colors up and down
your thighs. Together, we connected
the dots. There were no divisions,
no divisionism, only our bodies,
flying out of our skins.

## GARDEN OF THE PAINTER AT SAINT CLAIR, 1908
*~Henri-Edmond Cross*

Under the cool blue slats
of palm trees, a table
and two empty chairs;
an invitation to come and sit
in this luminous paradise,
perhaps with morning coffee
as the sun squeezes lemon
light through the scaffolding,
Or perhaps with a glass
of wine in late afternoon
as grapey shadows
lengthen, stain the ground.
There are purple and yellow
iris in the foreground, colors
laid down in long strokes,
the way the foliage slices
the light. We're not there,
of course, but we could be,
even if it's just the garden
of our dreams. Here, paint
has stopped time in its blue
and gold tracks. And these
flowers keep unfolding.

## DUSK AT LA BAIE DES ANGES, 1932
*~ Raoul Dufy*

Dufy studied *couleur-lumière*, the effect
of light on color, turned the Mediterranean
into a pool of flat cerulean. No wind riffles
the water; this is sea as satin tablecloth
or slab of marble. That smooth. That cool.
Here in Virginia, blue jays
have been interrupting my morning
with their imperious squawks.
Their feathers, the blue fire of the Côte d'Azur
in summer. In Dufy's oils, the sky sings
hyacinthine. There is no motion; even the lone
palm on the right hand side of the painting
holds its breath. The figures in the foreground
are poised, waiting for night to come down
and paint them midnight, cold steel, indigo. . . .

## CAP NÈGRE, 1909
### ~Henri-Edmond Cross

These short sharp brush strokes are exactly
the color of the pain radiating up
from my shredded ankle, ligaments shot
to hell and gone. Cap Nègre's in Saint-Clair,
near Saint-Tropez, where Cross and Signac
developed Divisionism. My ankle's divided
from the rest of my body, shooting out
sparks with every step. In Cross's charcoal
and watercolor on cream laid paper, the trees
and promontory vibrate, every brush stroke
licked with light. While my ankle explodes
in all the colors of the trees: wince blue,
livid magenta, jaundice.

## MODEL IN THE ARTIST'S STUDIO, 1928
*~ Raoul Dufy*

This model is zaftig, even hefty by today's standards,
fleshy thighs, round belly, ample curves. Bottom
heavy as a ripe pear. But she is *bien dans sa peau*,
doesn't go to Weight Watchers, had a café crème
this morning, broke her croissant into small pieces,
dabbed it with *confiture d'abricot*, little bits
of sun. She took pleasure in the moment.
So when Dufy posed her, arms behind
her head, solid hips jutting right, there she
was, delectable as an oyster, ready to be
consumed. And here we are in our imperfect
flesh, the dimpled arms, the parts that jiggle,
the great softening, as we succumb to gravity,
our last lover. So let's raise our arms above
our heads, let the world see the pudding bowl
our bellies have become. These hips have carried
babies, these thighs have walked many miles. This
is it; it's not going to get any better. So let's stand
in the cool light of this blue room naked as the day
we were born. Let's tip our breasts to the sun,
and love our unairbrushed surgically unaltered
exquisite bodies for what they are:
the houses that we live in.

## HOUSE BEHIND TREES, 1906-7
  ~ Georges Braque

*I want to go home*, my friend's mother says,
over and over, even though this is the house
she's lived in fifty-some years. Alzheimer's,
dementia; different patients, same story:
they want to go home. I wish I could send them
to this house behind the blue trees, with its solid
flattened space, bright primaries outlined in bold
strokes of cobalt. The rest of the colors run away
with themselves, the spectrum as playground.
Wouldn't we want to go there, too, return
to childhood's box of Crayolas, coloring the roof
yellow if we felt like it; the sky sea-green with clouds
swimming by like a school of fish. We could splash pink
wherever we wanted, eat marshmallows for dinner,
give up our naps, yell *oley oley in free*
as the shadows begin to twist and lengthen. . . .

## WOMEN PICKING OLIVES, 1889

*~Vincent Van Gogh*
*The oil that is extracted here from the most beautiful olives*
*in the world replaces butter. I had great misgivings*
*about this substitution. But I have tasted it in sauces*
*and, truthfully, there is nothing better.*
*~Jean Racine, "Lettres d'Uzès, 1661"*

And there's nothing better than old friends; no substitutes
will do. These women in their plain colored dresses remind
me of what I've lost, the friends who are not here. There's
nothing rational about this, why a woman on a ladder,
another reaching into the trees, a third with a pannier
would speak to me of loss, but there are spaces
between the branches where the dove-colored sky
bleeds through, and the path through the orchard
runs like a river, liquid brush strokes of clay, the field
ochre on both sides. The dead no longer need to feed
the body, decide between oil and butter for their bread.
They can slip between the next world and ours
if they want to, on the breath of the wind.
There's a ladder in this painting, but it doesn't reach
to heaven. Instead, it's the divide, the uncrossable
bridge, the message still on the answering machine.
Above the orchard, the sky is full of ashes of roses:
parentheses, ellipses, things we hold onto,
even as they slip away.

## ESPAGNOLE: HARMONIE EN BLEU, 1923
~Henri Matisse

Why shouldn't the dead go on speaking?
Here is a woman in a lace mantilla,
black fan snapped shut, bangles
on her wrists, arm resting on a table.
Around her neck, a choker of pearls.
She looks in my eyes straight as a shot
of Cognac. Her mouth parts slightly.
What is she trying to say? I have been
listening, hoping to hear my own dead friends:
Clare, Michèle, Adrianne. Snippets
come to me in birdsong, in gesture,
in the dark wing of a stranger's hair.
But it's like deciphering code, or reading
through water. The dead have their own
language. Are they restless, do they long
to come back, smell peonies in spring?
Or is being dead enough, the end of the story,
the book gently closing, and the conversation over?

## notes

"Walking with Jesus" is after a poem by David Kirby.
"Listen" is after Barbara Hamby's "Sonnets from the Psalms."
"Women" is after Dorianne Laux's "Men."
"Life" is after "Starfish" by Eleanor Lerman.
"Compare & Contrast" is for Martha Silano.
"Against Understatement" is for Mary Meriam.
"So, This Guy I Know" is for Ken Poyner.
"Why I Love Being Married to a Chemist" is after a poem
   by Andrea Potos.

## thanks

Many thanks to Marjorie Stelmach, Geri Rosenzweig, Ken Fifer, Dorothy Ryan, Barbara Reisner, and Kathleen Moser for their keen eyes and ears in looking at earlier versions of these poems, and to The Virginia Center for the Creative Arts for the gift of space and time to organize the manuscript. Also thanks to the Moulin à Nef, Auvillar, France, for the residency where many of these poems began. And thanks to my husband, Richard Crooker, for keeping down the fort at home which has allowed me to set off on these adventures.

# acknowledgements

| | |
|---|---|
| *The Alabama Literary Review* | "*Dusk at La Baie des Anges, 1932*" |
| | "*The Green Blouse, 1919*" |
| *Angle* (UK) | "Dreaming on Paper" |
| *The Anglican Theological Review* | "Pilgrims" |
| *The Christian Century* | "Le Nid des Anges" |
| *The Comstock Poetry Review* | "*Ink*" |
| *The Cumberland Poetry Review* | "Usage" |
| *Earth's Daughters* | "It Was the Night of the Full Moon" |
| | "The Beauty Tarp" |
| | "Compare & Contrast" |
| *Gargoyle* | "Sins of Omission" |
| | "Weather Systems" |
| | "Why I Love Being Married to a Chemist" |
| *The Houston Art Museum, ARTlines* | |
| | "*The Turning Road, l'Estaque, 1906*" |
| *The Innisfree Poetry Review* | "The Bossy Letter R" |
| | "*Live* or *Evil, Rats* or *Star*" |
| *Italian-Americana* | "*Sketch for 'le boneur de vivre'*" |
| | "Word Search" |
| *Journal of New Jersey Poets* | |
| | "*Figure Decorative Sur Fond Ornemental, 1925*" |
| *Kestrel* | "*Cap Nègre, 1909*" |
| *Kentucky Review* | "At the Moulin Pastelier" |
| *The MacGuffin* | "*La Mer Vue à Collioure, 1906*" |
| | "*The Jetty at Cassis, Opus 198, 1889*" |
| | "Auvillar" |
| | "Dictionary" |
| | "*Field with Wheat Stacks*" |
| *Mezzo Cammin* | "Fenestration" |
| | "Listen" |
| | "This American Life" |
| | "In King of Prussia" |
| | "Alpha/Omega" |
| *Miramar* | "The Recent Dead" |

| | |
|---|---|
| *Negative Capability* | "My Heart" |
| *Nimrod* | "Figs" |
| | "Scrimshaw" |
| | "*L'Atelier Rose, 1911*" |
| | "*Pansies, 1918-1919*" |
| *Oregon English* | "Your" |
| *Paterson Literary Review* | |

"So, This Guy I Know Challenges Me to Write a Poem"

| | |
|---|---|
| *Perspectives* | "Walking with Jesus" |
| | "Life" |
| *Poet Lore* | "*Odalisque avec Anémones, 1937*" |
| | "*Espagnole: Harmonie en Bleu, 1923*" |
| | "*Garden of the Painter at Saint Clair, 1908*" |
| *Rattle* | "Women" |
| *Raven Chronicles* | "*Seventeen Phrases You're Probably Saying Wrong*" |
| *St. Katherine Review* | "Les Boulangers" |
| *San Pedro Poetry Review* | "*Landscape with Stars, 1905-08*" |
| *Switched-on Gutenberg* | "Sixty-Five" |
| *US One Worksheets* | "Dixon-Ticonderoga" |
| *The Valparaiso Poetry Review* | "*Ears of Wheat, 1890*" |
| | "*Women Picking Olives, 1889*" |
| *Verse Wisconsin* | "Against Understatement" |
| | "*House Behind Trees, 1906-07*" |
| *Rock & Sling* | "Église Saint-Pierre" |

"*Figure Decorative Sur Fond Ornemental, 1925*" was runner-up for the 2014 New Jersey Poets Prize. "Figs," "*L'Atelier Rose, 1911*," and "*Pansies*" were finalists for the 2012 Pablo Neruda Poetry Prize from *Nimrod*. "Figs," "*L'Atelier Rose, 1911*," and "*Pansies, 1918-1919*" were nominated for the 2013 Pushcart Prize. "*House Behind Trees, 1906-07*" appeared in the anthology *Forgetting Home: Poems About Alzheimer's* (Barefoot Muse Press, 2013). "Litany of the Desk Drawer" appeared in *Wingbeats II* (Dos Gatos Press).

"Le Nid des Anges" is used by permission from *The Christian Century*.

# OTHER C&R PRESS TITLES

## FICTION

Spectrum
by Martin Ott

That Man in Our Lives
by Xu Xi

A History of the Cat In Nine Chapters or Less
by Anis Shivani

## SHORT FICTION

Notes From the Mother Tongue
by An Tran

The Protester Has Been Released
by Janet Sarbanes

## ESSAY AND CREATIVE NONFICTION

While You Were Gone
by Sybil Baker

Je suis l'autre: Essays and Interrogations
by Kristina Marie Darling

Death of Art
by Chris Campanioni

## POETRY

Imagine Not Drowning
by Kelli Allen

Collected Lies and Love Poems
by John Reed

Tall as You are Tall Between Them
by Annie Christain

The Couple Who Fell to Earth
by Michelle Bitting

## ANTHOLOGY

Zombies, Aliens, Cyborgs and the Ongoing Apocolypse
by Travis Denton and Katie Chaple

## CHAPBOOKS

Notes from the Negro Side of the Moon
by Earl Braggs

A Hunger Called Music: A Verse History in Black Music
by Meredith Nnoka

Printed in the USA
CPSIA information can be obtained
at www.ICGtesting.com
LVHW041940010923
756974LV00010B/828